My First
Picture
Dictionary

cat

apple

butterfly

Aa

airplane

An **airplane** is a flying machine with wings that carries people and things.

alphabet

An **alphabet** is the letters that are used in writing, arranged in a special order.

ambulance

An **ambulance** is a special van that is used to take people to hospital when they are hurt or sick.

Nee naa! Nee naa!

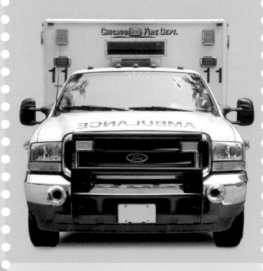

angry

If you are **angry**, you feel very upset and annoyed.

animal

An **animal** is something that lives and moves around. A plant is not an animal. Cats, robins, spiders, and goldfish are all animals.

apple

An **apple** is a round, juic fruit that grows on a tre Its skin can be green, red, or yellow.

Bb

basket

A **basket** is a container used to store and carry things.

bee

A **bee** is an insect with wings. Bees make honey.

ball

A **ball** is a round object used in games. You throw, catch, hit, or kick a ball.

bat

A **bat** is a piece of wood that is used to hit a ball in a game.

beetle

A **beetle** is an insect that has hard, shiny wings.

banana

A **banana** is a long fruit with a thick, yellow skin.

bed

A **bed** is something you lie down and sleep on.

bicycle

A **bicycle** is a machine you ride. It has two wheels and pedals.

bird

A **bird** is an animal with wings, feathers, and a beak. Most birds can fly.

book

A **book** is made up of pages held together inside a cover.

box

A **box** is used to keep things in. Most boxes are made of cardboard.

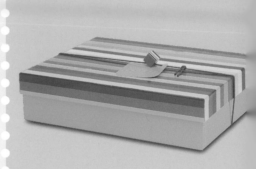

body

The **body** of a person or an animal is every part of them.

bottle

A **bottle** holds liquids. Bottles are usually made of glass or plastic.

bowl

A **bowl** is a deep dish that holds food like soup, breakfast cereal, or fruit.

boy

A **boy** is a child who will grow up to be a man.

bread

Bread is a food made with flour. It is baked in an oven.

bucket

A bucket is used to carry liquid.

butterfly

A butterfly is an insect that has four large wings.

broccoli

Broccoli is a green vegetable.

bulldozer

A bulldozer is a big machine that pushes rocks out of the way.

brush

A brush has lots of stiff hairs or wires. Most brushes have a handle.

bus

A bus is a long vehicle with seats inside to carry people around.

button

A button is a small object that you sew on to clothes to fasten them.

a b c d e f g h i j k l m n o p q r s t u v w x y z

Cc

carrot

A **carrot** is a long, orange vegetable that grows under the ground.

caterpillar

A **caterpillar** looks like a worm with legs. It turns into a butterfly or moth.

cake

A **cake** is a sweet food. It is made by mixing butter, sugar, eggs, and flour and baking it in an oven.

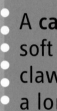

cat

A **cat** is an animal with soft fur, sharp claws, and a long tail. People keep small cats as pets.

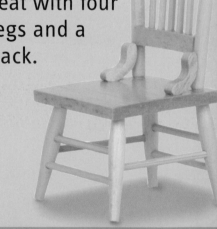

chair

A **chair** is a seat with four legs and a back.

car

A **car** is a machine with four wheels and an engine.

catch

When you **catch** something, you take hold of it while it is moving.

cheese

Cheese is a food made from milk.

child

A **child** is a young boy or girl. When there is more than one child, they are called children.

chocolate

Chocolate is a sweet, brown food made from cocoa beans.

clock

A **clock** is a machine that shows you what time it is.

clothes

Clothes are the things that people wear, such as pants, dresses, and shirts.

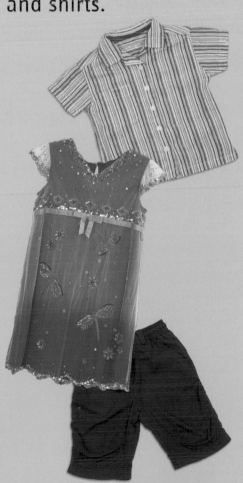

clown

A **clown** is someone who says and does funny things to make people laugh.

color

Red, blue, and yellow are **colors**. By mixing them together, you get other colors.

comb

A **comb** is a piece of plastic or metal that has lots of thin teeth. You use a comb to fix your hair.

a b c d e f g h i j k l m n o p q r s t u v w x y z

ABCDEFGHIJKLMNOP

computer

A **computer** is a machine that stores information and can work things out.

crawl

When you **crawl**, you move around on your hands and knees.

cry

When you **cry**, tears fall from your eyes.

cow

A **cow** is a large female farm animal that produces milk. The male animal is called a bull. The baby is called a calf.

Moo!

crocodile

A **crocodile** is an animal with sharp teeth, short legs, and a long tail.

cucumber

A **cucumber** is a long, green vegetable.

crown

A **crown** is a kind of hat, usually worn by kings and queens. It's often made of gold or silver.

cup

A **cup** is a small, round container with a handle. You drink from a cup.

Dd

dish
A **dish** is a bowl for serving food.

dog
A **dog** is an animal that barks. Dogs are often kept as pets.

dice
Dice are small cubes that have a different number of spots on each side.

doctor
A **doctor** takes care of people who are sick or hurt and helps them to get better.

dinosaur
Dinosaurs were large animals that lived on Earth millions of years ago.

donkey
A **donkey** is a furry animal that looks like a small horse with long ears.

Ee

egg

Birds, fish, snakes, and lizards live inside **eggs** until they are big enough to hatch out.

envelope

An **envelope** is a paper cover for a letter or a card.

eagle

An **eagle** is a large bird with big wings, a curved beak, and sharp claws.

elephant

An **elephant** is a large, gray animal that has big ears and a long nose, called a trunk.

exercise

When you **exercise**, you move your body to keep fit.

ear

Your **ears** are on each side of your head. You hear with your ears.

eye

Your **eyes** are on your face. You see with your eyes.

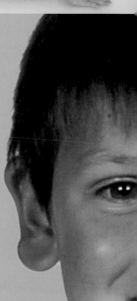

F f

family
Your **family** is the group of people that are closest to you. Your Mom, Dad, brothers, and sisters are all part of your family.

feather
Birds have **feathers** on their bodies to keep them warm and dry. Feathers can also help birds fly.

face
Your **face** is the front part of your head. Your eyes, nose, and mouth are all part of your face.

finger
Your **fingers** are part of your hand. Each hand has four fingers and a thumb.

farm
A **farm** is a place where farmers grow food and raise animals.

fire
A **fire** is the hot, bright flames and smoke made when something is burning.

fire truck

A **fire truck** is a special vehicle with a ladder and water hose. Firefighters use fire trucks to drive to fires and put them out.

Nee naa!

Nee naa!

flower

A **flower** is part of a plant. Flowers are often perfumed and brightly colored.

fork

A **fork** has sharp prongs and a handle. You use a small fork for eating and a big fork for digging in the garden.

food

Food is something you eat to keep you strong and healthy.

frog

A **frog** is a small animal that lives in ponds and damp places.

fish

A **fish** is an animal that lives in water. Fish are covered in scales and have gills for breathing under water.

fruit

A **fruit** is the part of a plant that holds the seeds. Lots of fruits, like apples and grapes, are juicy and good to eat.

Gg

giraffe
A **giraffe** is a tall animal with long legs and a very long neck.

goat
A **goat** is an animal with long hair and horns on its head.

game
A **game** is something you play for fun. Bat and ball is a game.

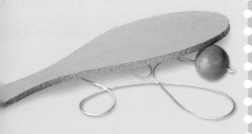

grape
A **grape** is a small, purple or green fruit that grows in bunches. Grapes are used to make wine.

gate
A **gate** is a kind of door in a wall, fence, or hedge.

girl
A **girl** is a child who will grow up to be a woman.

grow
When somebody or something **grows**, they get bigger.

a b c d e f g h i j k l m n o p q r s t u v w x y z

Hh

head

Your **head** is the part of your body that is above your neck.

hop

You **hop** when you jump up and down on one leg.

half

A **half** is one of two pieces that are equal in size.

helicopter

A **helicopter** is a flying machine with spinning blades that let it take off straight up from the ground and hover. Helicopters don't have wings.

horse

A **horse** is a big animal with hooves. People ride horses and use them to pull loads.

hammer

A **hammer** is a tool for pounding nails into wood.

house

A **house** is a building where people live.

I i

idea

An **idea** is something you think of.

ice

Ice is made when water freezes. Ice is very cold and hard.

ice cream

Ice cream is a sweet, creamy, frozen food.

insects

An **insect** is a small animal with six legs. Many insects have wings. Butterflies, flies, and beetles are all insects.

J j

jar

Jars are usually made of glass. They are used for keeping foods, like jam, fresh.

jewel

A **jewel** is a beautiful, sparkling stone. Some jewels, like diamonds, cost a lot of money.

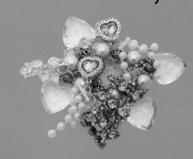

jigsaw puzzle

A **jigsaw puzzle** is made from lots of pieces that you fit together to make a picture.

K k

king

A **king** is a man who is born to rule a country. A queen's husband is also called a king.

juice

Juice is the liquid that comes out of fruit when you squeeze it.

key

A **key** is a specially shaped piece of metal that is used to lock or unlock a door.

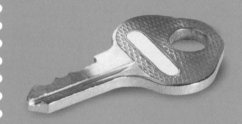

jump

When you **jump**, you lift both feet off the ground and move suddenly up into the air.

kick

When you **kick** something, you hit it with your foot.

knife

A **knife** is a tool used for cutting. Most knives have a handle and a long, sharp metal blade.

L l

lamp

A lamp gives you light. You can move a lamp around and switch it on and off.

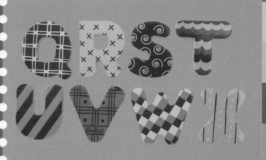

letter

A letter is a sign you use to write words. A, m, and z are all letters.

ladder

A ladder is used for climbing up high. Ladders are made of metal or wood.

leaf

A leaf is one of the flat, green parts of a plant or tree.

A letter is also a message that you write on paper to someone.

lamb

A lamb is a young sheep that is still with its mother.

lemon

A lemon is a juicy, yellow fruit with a sour taste.

lion

A lion is a big, wild cat. Lions live in Africa and India.

Mm

map

A **map** is a drawing that shows you where places are, so you can find your way around.

medicine

You take **medicine** when you are sick to make you well again.

man

A **man** is a grown-up male person.

mask

A **mask** is something that you wear to cover your face. People wear masks to change the way they look.

milk

Milk is a white liquid that mother animals make to feed their babies with. Many people drink cows' milk.

mirror

A **mirror** is a sheet of special glass that you can see yourself in.

money

Money is the bills and coins that you use to buy things.

mountain

A **mountain** is a very high piece of land or rock.

mushroom

A **mushroom** is a plant that looks like a little umbrella. You can eat some mushrooms.

moon

The **moon** shines in the sky at night. It moves slowly around the Earth once a month.

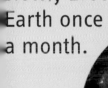

mouse

A **mouse** is a small, furry animal with a long tail. Mice have sharp, front teeth for gnawing food.

music

Music is the sound that people make when they sing and play instruments.

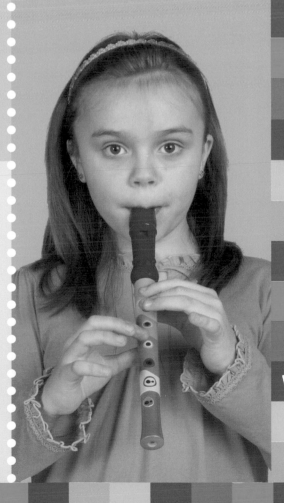

motorcycle

A **motorcycle** has two wheels and an engine.

mug

A **mug** is a large, straight cup with a handle. You drink hot drinks from a mug.

a b c d e f g h i j k l m n o p q r s t u v w x y z

Nn

net

A **net** is made from pieces of string or thread tied together with holes in between. Nets are used for catching fish and also in games like tennis and football.

number

Numbers tell you how many of something you have. 3 and 100 are both numbers.

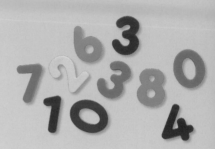

needle

A **needle** is a small, thin piece of metal used for sewing. It is sharp at one end and has a hole for thread at the other.

nurse

A **nurse** is a person who takes care of people who are sick or hurt. Nurses often work in hospitals.

nest

A **nest** is the home that animals like birds and mice make for their babies.

nose

Your **nose** is part of your face. You use it for breathing and smelling.

Oo

oven

An **oven** is the compartment in a stove where you roast or bake food.

opposite

An **opposite** is completely different. The opposite of full is empty.

orange

An **orange** is a round, juicy fruit with thick, orange peel.

owl

An **owl** is a bird that hunts for small animals at night. It has big eyes to help it see in the dark.

Pp

paint

Paint is a liquid that you put on to things to change the color.

paper

Paper is a very thin material used for drawing and writing.

parrot

A **parrot** is a bird with brightly colored feathers and a sharp, curved beak. Some parrots can talk.

pencil

A **pencil** is a long, thin stick of wood with black or colored lead in the middle. Pencils are used for writing and drawing.

pet

A **pet** is a tame animal that you take care of in your home. Cats, dogs, and hamsters are often kept as pets.

penguin

A **penguin** is a black-and-white sea bird that lives on cold coastlines. Penguins can't fly. They use their wings to swim.

pen

A **pen** is something you use to write or draw with in ink.

pig

A **pig** is an animal with a fat body, short legs, and a curly tail.

pirate

A **pirate** is a sailor who attacks and robs other sailors at sea.

plate

A **plate** is a flat dish that you put food on.

present

A **present** is something special that you give to someone to make them happy.

play

When you **play**, you have fun with your friends and join in games. Children and baby animals love to play with toys.

pumpkin

A **pumpkin** is a large fruit with orange skin.

plant

A **plant** is a living thing that grows in soil or water. Trees, flowers, and grass are all plants.

puppet

A **puppet** is a toy figure. You move a puppet by pulling strings or by putting your hand inside it.

a b c d e f g h i j k l m n o p q r s x y z

A
B
C
D
E
F
G
H
I
J
K
L
M
N
O
P
Q
R
S
T
U
V
W
X
Y
Z

Qq Rr

rainbow

A **rainbow** is an arch of bright colors that you see when the sun shines through rain.

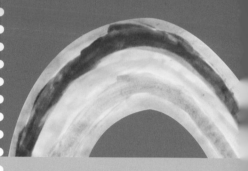

queen

A **queen** is a woman who is born to rule a country.

rabbit

A **rabbit** is a small, furry animal with long ears and a fluffy, white tail.

read

When you **read**, you can understand words that are written down.

question

A **question** is what you ask when you want to know something.

rain

Rain is lots of little drops of water that fall from the clouds.

rhinoceros

A **rhinoceros** is a big animal with tough, leathery skin and horns on its head.

robot

A **robot** is a machine that can do some of the jobs that people do.

S s

saw

A **saw** is a tool with sharp, metal teeth for cutting through wood.

rocket

A **rocket** is the part of a spacecraft that pushes it high into space.

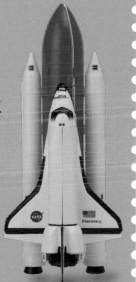

sandwich

A **sandwich** is made of two slices of bread with a filling, such as cheese or ham, between them.

scissors

A pair of **scissors** is a tool used to cut paper or cloth. Scissors have two sharp blades and two handles.

ruler

A **ruler** is a long, flat piece of wood or plastic that is used for drawing lines and measuring length.

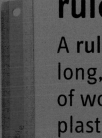

saucepan

A **saucepan** is a deep, metal cooking pot with a handle and usually a lid.

shape

The **shape** of something is its outline or the way it looks on the outside.

shark

A **shark** is a big fish. Some sharks have very sharp teeth and can attack people.

shoe

You wear **shoes** on your feet to protect them.

snake

A **snake** has a long body and no legs. Its skin is made of scales.

sheep

A **sheep** is an animal with a thick, woolly coat.

sleep

When you **sleep**, you close your eyes and rest.

snowman

A **snowman** is shaped like a person and made out of snow.

shell

A **shell** is a hard covering around something. Shellfish and nuts have shells.

smile

When you **smile**, the corners of your mouth turn up. A smile means you feel happy.

sock

You wear **socks** on your feet to keep them warm.

spade

A **spade** is a tool used to dig holes in the ground. It has a long handle and a flat, metal end.

squirrel

A **squirrel** is a small, furry animal that lives in trees. It has a bushy tail and eats nuts.

strawberry

A **strawberry** is a soft, sweet red fruit with seeds on it.

spider

A **spider** is a small animal with eight legs. Spiders spin webs to catch insects for food.

star

A **star** is a small, bright light in the sky. You can see stars on a clear, dark night. A star is also a shape with five or more points.

sun

The **Sun** shines in the sky and gives the Earth light and heat. It is a star and the Earth moves around it.

spoon

A **spoon** has a long handle and a round part at one end. You use a spoon to eat foods like soup and cereals.

starfish

A **starfish** is an animal with five arms that lives in the ocean. It looks like a star.

swan

A **swan** is a large bird with a long neck. It lives on rivers and lakes.

a b c d e f g h i j k l m n o p q r s t

T t

telephone

A **telephone** is a machine you use to talk to someone in another place.

thermometer

You use a **thermometer** to find out how hot or cold something is.

table

A **table** is a piece of furniture with legs and a flat top. You can eat at a table.

tail

An animal's **tail** grows at the end of its body.

tent

A **tent** is a shelter made out of a piece of cloth stretched over metal poles. You use a tent for camping.

tiger

A **tiger** is a big, wild cat with orange fur and black stripes. Wild tigers are rare, but some still live in India and China.

tomato

A **tomato** is a soft, red, round fruit that you often eat in salads.

toothbrush

You use a **toothbrush** and toothpaste to keep your teeth clean.

tractor

A **tractor** is a farm vehicle with big back wheels to pull things.

tool

A **tool** is something you hold in your hands to help you do things. Saws, wrenches, and spades are all tools.

towel

A **towel** is a piece of soft, thick cloth that you dry yourself with.

tree

A **tree** is a tall plant with leaves, branches, and a thick stem of wood called a trunk.

toy

A **toy** is something a child plays with. Dolls, kites, and train sets are all toys.

truck

A **truck** is a strong vehicle that moves things to other places.

a b c d e f g h i j k l m n o p q r s t u v w x y z

Uu Vv

vase

A **vase** is a kind of container that is used to hold cut flowers.

umbrella

An **umbrella** keeps you dry when it rains.

vacuum cleaner

A **vacuum cleaner** is a machine that sucks up dust and dirt.

vegetable

A **vegetable** is a plant that can be eaten raw or cooked. Carrots, cabbages, and onions are all vegetables.

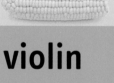

uniform

Some people wear **uniform** to show what job they do or which school they go to.

violin

A **violin** is a musical instrument made of wood. You play it using a bow.

Ww

wheel

Wheels are round and they can turn. Bicycles, cars, and trains all have wheels.

watch

A **watch** is a small clock that you wear on your wrist. It tells you what time it is.

woman

A **woman** is a grown-up female person.

water

Water is a clear liquid found in rivers and oceans. Water also comes out of faucets.

Xx

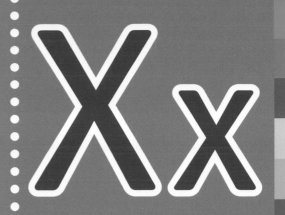

x-ray

An **X-ray** is a picture that lets a doctor see inside your body.

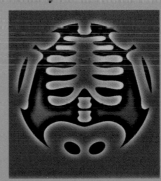

xylophone

A **xylophone** is a musical instrument with a row of wooden bars.

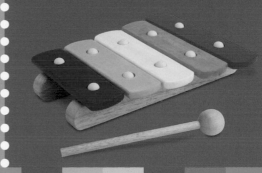

a b c d e f g h i j k l m n o p q r s t u v w x y z

Y y

Z z

yogurt

Yogurt is a food made from milk. It is often mixed with fruit.

yacht

A **yacht** is a boat with sails. Most yachts also have an engine.

yolk

The **yolk** is the yellow or orange middle part of an egg.

zebra

A **zebra** looks like a horse with black and white stripes. Zebras live in Africa.

yawn

When you **yawn**, you open your mouth wide and breathe out noisily.

yo-yo

A **yo-yo** is a round toy that you roll up and down on a string.

zipper

A **zipper** joins two pieces of material together. A zipper has teeth that lock together when you zip it up.

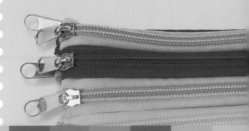